If You Can Identify It You Can Hogtie It

Marc Murchison

authorHOUSE®

AuthorHouse™
1663 Liberty Drive
Bloomington, IN 47403
www.authorhouse.com
Phone: 1-800-839-8640

First published by AuthorHouse 11/20/2010

ISBN: 978-1-4520-5577-0 (sc)
ISBN: 978-1-4520-5576-3 (e)

Library of Congress Control Number: 2010911219

Printed in the United States of America

This book is printed on acid-free paper.

PREFACE

THANK YOU FOR THE PURCHASE OF MY BOOK

Hi folks. My name is Marc Murchison, the author of this book. I want to thank you for my book. I pray that there will be numerous things that will help you begin to identify with how these disorders affect you. In my book you may read some things that seem to sound the same that I have written in my other chapters along the way. Well there is a reason for this. It is important to keep certain words upfront and fresh in your mind. I guess you can look at it like a chain. Some chapters are linked together, link by link. After you have read this book, please read it again. This will help you pick up on things that you may have missed and soon you will be able to understand how some changes in your own life will help you begin to fight the dreadful battle between you and anxiety/panic disorders.

This book will cover several different topics such as hope, healing, prayer, depression, stress, and addictions. In this book I will share some stories with you that you may find very touching and very helpful to your everyday life. I was inspired to write this book after I got a double dose of these disorders. In this book you will begin to see how I was able to identify with my disorders. I had the blessing in the past to help others also learning how to (IDENTIFY IT AND HOG TIE IT) always remember sometimes it's the simplest things that help us the most. I believe that if you will begin to gain some knowledge of just what these disorders are about, you will be able to take control very soon. No big fancy medical words. So please take what you can use from my book and apply it. God bless you on your journey to feeling better and moving on with your life. I know you can do it I did . So have many others in the past. Just a reminder that you are not the only one that has had to deal with these disorders. There are millions of people that have generalized anxiety/panic disorders. Listen if you just choose to lay down and take it, oh poor pitiful me. Then that is all you will ever be is just poor pitiful you. Read my book so you can get back to being yourself again.

Prayer was so important in my journey to

a better and more healthier way of life. Share this book with your loved ones so they may also understand how you are feeling and help you on your way to recovery. Please don't give your book away. Always keep it so you can refer back to if you should experience some tough days. I myself, refer back to my own book as well. Just a few days ago, stress started moving in on me, I was having a few rough days with the anxiety disorder so, I referred back to the chapter, (BE THANKFUL FOR THE GOOD DAYS) this helped me realize that most of the days of the month were great so, I kept marching on and I have felt fine ever since. People quit spending your money on quick fix books and cds. It's going to take you a little time and effort to identify with these disorders. So put a smile on your face and go do some hog tying. When you purchase this self help book, I will be donating a % of the cost of the book to a cancer hospital for kids. You will be helping yourself and some precious kids as well. Thank you for giving back. God bless you today for helping.

TABLE OF CONTENTS

ANXIETY AND ME

Well all I can tell you in my early stages of these nightmares; of chemical imbalance disorders, sometimes it was hard for me to tell the difference between a panic attack or an anxiety attack. The fear you feel is so overwhelming at the time. An anxiety attack can last for hours or sometimes days. A panic attack seems to be over in just a few minutes. Those few minutes can be pure hell on wheels. Later on as you read along in my book, you will start to notice what helped me and others in the past.

We are all different and that's why some people experience general anxiety disorder in a different way than others. My symptoms were mild depression. I would feel my teeth clamping together and at night when I would sleep I would grind my teeth {Note: If you are doing this you can ask your dentist to make you a rubber mouthpiece and this will save your teeth from getting worn down} I would feel hot, sweaty, and clammy. Sometimes I would feel like I was burning up and fighting to get some air. It was like a hot flash. Wow that was not a good feeling at all. Then my stomach would hurt and I felt like I was going to just throw up right then. My heart would pound and my chest would tighten up as if I was having a heart attack. I would be so nervous I could not stand it. The fear began to grip me like a vise.

I felt so scared I thought something else was wrong in body. I would become dizzy and I felt that my normal balance was off, but it is that out of body experience that was the kicker. Do you feel like this sometimes? Like your standing in one place, but you feel like your body is out to the side of you. Man this was so weird and when I would walk I felt I was walking to one side (WOO !!). That's not any fun at all! I would also feel pressure behind my right eye and some blurred vision. I tried to blame this on a sinus infection and went to see a specialist and he checked everything including the muscles behind my eyes, but said everything looked fine. I bet you feel nervous and jittery often too. Don't you? Come on tell the truth.

It feels like you just can't get rid of this overwhelming, skin crawling, nerve racking feeling.

It just lingers on and on. My brain would play tricks on me. Like a couple of times I literally felt like I was going to die that instant. It just overtook me and felt so real. What agony. I felt like I got A double dose of these anxiety/panic disorders. It also gave me a social type phobia, as it does to many people. I will explain this later on for you, and did I mention {INSOMNIA}? Which means not being able to sleep and soon you begin to start feeling run down more and more each day with having these disorders. It's so important to get plenty of rest. When you do without rest and a goodnight's sleep you begin to feel stressed out and this can make your situation even worse day to day, so remember to check with your doctor and try to find some non-addicting sleep medicine until you learn how to relax and begin to deal with your anxiety problems. As for me it was a natural sleep-aide, melotonin and prayer.

I believe in prayer and this helped me along with having hope and believing in healing. { Thank you Jesus } You know that these anxiety attacks just aggravated the heck out of me, but the more frequent I had these attacks I began to start to identify when one was starting to come on and this is when I began to work on my ways to prepare myself for this battle. You know what? They began to work again and again. Wow, how exciting and you will soon feel this way too! See as you are reading this your mind is on the book not on the anxiety as you are hoping for a way to cope with your problem. (Sorry folks there is no quick fix in here, just powerful information to help you live a more calmer and peaceful and certainly a more fruitful life).

{ **HOPE** } Please remember this word, because it can change your life, it changed mine. A doctor of 44 years of practice told me when he diagnosed me with these disorders, said that no one has ever died or been seriously hurt do to a anxiety or panic attack to his knowledge. He told me that millions of Americans live with disorders every day of their lives and function just fine with the right type of medicine or therapy. Man did I want to here that. I thought it was the end for me, but when he told me that it gave me { **HOPE** }. That's all I needed, because I'm a fighter. I have been a small business man all my life and when you own a business you learn a little about fighting. Like, your competition or just keeping your business afloat in the tough times.

Try to remember that knowledge is power and it can get you way ahead of the rough times. I have experienced in the past that it's the fear of not knowing what is wrong with you or what to do that seems to grip you like a vise. As you begin to learn what to look for you will then identify with it more and more. This helps to start reducing the fear factor.

The bible says in 1 JOHN 4:4 "Greater is he that is in you, than he that is in the world. Thank you Jesus!

PSALM 119:50 " This is my comfort in my affliction, for your word has given me life".

You can find hope, comfort, healing, and salvation in Jesus Christ Amen!

So please keep reading and get ready to start feeling the hope, healing and happiness that you well deserve.

God bless you on your journey to great health…..

TELL THEM ABOUT IT

Hey folks. One of the most important things to do is to tell everyone you know about this diagnosis. Wow, after six doctors, a medical test nightmare and several thousands of dollars later, I finally was told what was wrong with me and at that moment my mind raced and all I could think about was how will I tell my family and friends? Will they think I'm a nut case? I already knew that they were wondering why I was staying shut up in my home, but they knew I felt uneasy when they would come and visit me or if I went to visit them.

Sometimes I would just get in my truck and leave, as this disorder caused me to have a social phobia. My mind would race and I would think to myself, will I be able to run my business or is it over or will I be on disability. Man how will I deal with my customers? I just felt doomed and washed up on the banks. Well I have good news, telling them was the best thing I have ever done. It helped them, help me by trying to understand what to do. Like giving me space and not feeling funny when I said I must go now. Also, they did not enable me, by running to my every beck and call. What was so funny is that a lot of them had experienced some of the same feelings I was having at different times of their lives and we would sometimes talk about it. This helped a lot to know someone else could understand what I was feeling. **NOTE:** When I would talk to someone about a panic attack in my early stages it would bring on an attack or almost throw me into one, because I was getting close to the fear of the other attacks. You should try to talk about this often so it will move you further and further away from the fear. Then I was amazed when I told my customers about my disorder. You would not believe how many of them have this same problem.

Time and time again we shared our stories about this whole big Anxiety/Panic/Phobia disorder business.

Man it felt great that so many others understood what I'm feeling and to see them moving on with their lives each day. Now I'm blessed to help others and have helped many with this awful feeling of dread and destruction that has come upon them. Just the other day I met a new customer and after talking with her a bit I could tell she was feeling depressed, somewhat scared, and jittery. So I started talking about my book and she asked what it was about? When I told her she got so excited and she said. " I have been dealing with panic attacks lately and feeling really depressed due to a bad marriage that consisted of physical assault to her along with some pretty overwhelming other things." You know she is a prime example of a wonderful person. She has a great job, nice home and seemed to be a wonderful parent also. She told me that she always seems somewhat depressed and feels that she's not happy with herself most of the time.

She felt that she's a giver and she seemed to always get taken advantage of. As we talked for around two hours I felt that there was something else that bothering her and as I shared some of what I have learned and gods word with her. I told her about a woman that was hurting as she had been taken advantage of when she was at a young age.(think you know what I mean now) Suddenly she hung her head and then looked me square in the eye with hers full of small teardrops, she didn't have to say anymore. She told me she trusted someone and they betrayed her, hurt her, and stole her joy. Man why is it the good ones that get the bad apples! God bless her. She then told me with a smile "I feel better". I thought I was the only one going through something bad.

I said, "No way sis there is a lot of us that have trouble dealing with things that happened in our past". I told her to just be honest with yourself, love yourself and don't be afraid to tell others what you feel and what your going through they will probably share some things about their life as well. You can help yourself and help them feel better along the way.

See just let it out refuse to let it imprison you. Don't live in the past, live in the future. The more you discuss it the better you will feel. The bible says in JOHN 8:32 "And ye shall know the truth, and the truth shall make you free". The word of god is truth. See JOHN 17:17 "Once you know the truth concerning healing in god's redemptive plan, then you can begin to exercise faith and expect the promises of god to manifest in you and they will rejoice".

The bible says in REVALATION 12:11 "And they overcame him by the blood of the lamb, and by the word of their testimony". **NOTE:** When your healing manifests itself and you recover and have the opportunity to testify to the grace of the lord-Do It ! The lord wants you to give glory to him for what he has done and it will also serve to help build faith in someone else who has need. Amen and Amen.

TEST YOURSELF

TEST YOURSELF TO SEE WHAT YOU HAVE LEARNED

_____

_____

_____

_____

_____

_____

_____

_____

_____

_____

_____

_____

_____

_____

_____

_____

_____

_____

_____

_____

_____

_____

_____

"(B)" IS FOR BOOGIE AND SPLIT

Wow! Now here is a phrase you can all use and sound so cool when you say it. Just for fun lets work on a fun saying with these words that would have been said 70's or 80's, here it goes man "I'm going to put it in "B" for boogie and split" is that cool dude? Ha, Ha now that was cool. See it feels good to have a little fun! Think of some lines you can say when you have time. Little exercises like these can get your mind off a lot of negative thoughts and put a smile on your face. Hey take a trip down memory lane in whatever era you grew up in.

Well we had some fun heck why should we be serious all the time? That's probably what is wrong with us these days! Like when we see an old friend and ask them "What's been going on with you lately?" They usually reply "Oh just been working" what is sad is that we reply back the same way. I'm guilty of this, but for some time now I have been saying "Just goofing off". I'm getting back to what I enjoy doing like fishing, camping, cookouts, music etc. and boy does it feel great. So start working on the things you love to do (make some time for you). Yes we all have to work, but not all the time and if you do have to work all the time then you might want to start looking for ways to reduce your debt. Now think about what you love to do and make some time to go and do it! Just learn to relax you only live once. So when you have a chance put it in "B" for boogie and split away from all that hard work.

Now we will talk about how sometimes you should not put yourself in uneasy places, unless you are working on Behavioral Therapy Techniques. Like if some friends want you to go to a concert, a movie or a big night out on the town. Maybe they just want to come over and hang out. You know there are times you are just not going to feel like doing some of these things until you get a better handle on these disorders. (Like I said earlier in Chapter 1 TELL THEM ABOUT IT).

It's so important for everyone you are close to or work with to know about the type of disorder you have. However, it is great to get out and have some social fun time. This sure helps with depression it's not good to be cooped up all the time. You will learn your limitations soon enough. I ventured out one day and rode with a friend of mine to go fix a truck and about half way there I calmly told him to turn around and please take me home as I felt uneasy panicky. See right there I put it in "B" for boogie and split. My sister has this disorder as well and she told me the other day she went with our other sister to visit a friend across town, as she was riding along with my sister that was driving and playing the radio too loud. She said she felt nervous and agitated, then asked her to turn it down a little. When they got to the friends house she was feeling really bad then and the friend asked her what was wrong and she said I feel like I'm having a panic attack! Her friend asked would you like to go lie down? She said I have them too sometimes and I know how you feel. See here she put herself in an uneasy place to far from home, but thank god the friend knew just what she was feeling and tried her best to make my sister feel safe. **NOTE:** My sister was told she had this disorder a short time ago. She is still working on the techniques to identify with it. She is doing well and has come along way. God bless her. Unlike myself , I have to identify with how this disorder makes me feel sometimes and have harnessed a lot of the nervousness and panicky feelings. I now ride along with others and go to movies, work, camping, cookouts, go shopping, play my guitar and sing songs with other people etc.

There are still some days when I know that It's just not a good day for some of these things. So on most of those days I do put it in "B" for boogie and split. I call these "Identity Days" or "Time to myself Days". I just relax and let it take run it's course. I believe whether you have anxiety or panic disorders or not everyone feels overwhelmed some days and when that happens, It's time to get away from it all and just relax. If you choose to relax don't feel guilty, tomorrow is another day and life will go on. Remember, the more you learn about these disorders and start facing them head on, you will soon learn that there won't be a lot of those "B" for boogie and split days. Just good ole, I feel great days. You will begin to identify with effects that these

Disorders have on you and the closer to them you get the more you will feel in control of them and you will be able to prepare yourself on what to do and over time it will seem they are fading away and becoming weaker as you grow stronger over harnessing the effects of them. So if you don't feel like going don't go! It's your body, be in total control. If you should be caught in an uneasy place (Just put it in "B" for boogie and split).

The bible tells us in ISAIAH: 41:10

"So do not fear, for I am with you; Do not be dismayed, for I am your god. I will strengthen you and help you, I will uphold you with my righteous right hand".

GOD BLESS YOU, GOOD HEALTH AND KEEP THE FAITH!

TEST YOURSELF

TEST YOURSELF TO SEE WHAT YOU HAVE LEARNED

_____
_____
_____
_____
_____
_____
_____
_____
_____
_____
_____
_____
_____
_____
_____
_____
_____
_____
_____
_____
_____

STRESS IS A MESS

You know it seems almost everyone around us is stressed out these days due to our bad economy and changes in our society. It's so sad at how many people have lost their jobs and how they are losing their homes to boot. Having to change your lifestyle is not so much fun either. It can be hard to get back to living simple. You know over time I have talked to so many people about stress and I do believe that there are may ways to control this mess of stress.

So here are some things you can do to relieve stress.

REDUCE SOME DEBT

WORK ON YOUR RELATIONSHIPS WITH YOUR SPOUSE OR CHILDREN

EXERCISE AND EAT HEALTHY

GET PLENTY OF REST

FORGIVE YOURSELF AND FORGIVE
OTHERS

HAVE FAMILY TIME

FIND A HOBBY

LEARN TO LOVE AND RESPECT
YOURSELF AND OTHERS

PRAYER AND BIBLE STUDY

Hey, I have heard it said many times ("Live
the American Dream") What they fail to tell you
is that it cost a fortune to own a big house or a
fancy car and not to mention the credit card debt.
Hey please don't get me wrong, it's ok to have
nice things, but you may want to make sure you
have the funds to pay for them. Too much debt
can become destruction and when destruction
hits here comes the stress! Most of us have heard
this said "Look they are trying to keep up with
the Jones's" I have never met the Jones's so I don't
know if they are doing well or not, but please
don't be dismayed you can still live the American

Dream It's called "FREEDOM" Freedom to achieve your goals and enjoy a more fruitful life. Please don't wait until you are to old to do the things you really love. If you are a senior citizen, hey the sky's the limit. You have worked hard, now go and enjoy the things you love to do. So today folks just lean over and turn the stress level knob down and maybe you will be singing "I can see clearly now the stress is gone". Maybe you could take that vacation you have been thinking about or get back to that hobby you loved so much. Yea I know you may be saying, I just don't have the desire to do any of those things, because I am scared and depressed and this fear I feel inside has overwhelmed me! Just remember in time it will get better as you start to change some things in your life. Hey, why sit and worry, when there is not a darn thing you can do about it. Just work on reducing stress and you will soon see how much better you feel in the days to come.

If you do the same things today, as you did yesterday, you will have the same results. So set a plan of attack and stay with it. stress can cause depression and this leads to anxiety and having them awful panic attacks. Learn to live your life one day at a time. God Bless You.

Remember: Lose the stress and fix the mess!

The Bible says in :Romans 13:8 "Let no debt

remain outstanding, except the continuing debt to love one another, for he who loves his fellow man has fulfilled the law. Wow, I wish everyone had this debt.

The Bible says in Matthew 6:27 "Who of you by worrying, can add a single hour to your life"

Friends just ask Jesus to help you today and accept him. Show him you are serious and he will show you that he is faithful and hears your every prayer.

TEST YOURSELF

TEST YOURSELF TO SEE WHAT
YOU HAVE LEARNED

_____

_____

_____

_____

_____

_____

_____

_____

_____

_____

_____

_____

_____

_____

_____

_____

_____

_____

_____

_____

_____

_____

MILD DEPRESSION

Well folks, this subject is a very touchy one for me because there are so many types of depression. I can only share with you the type of depression I encounter sometimes. Depression has such a wide span from being mild to very severe at times. I recommend that you seek professional help with severe depression. I will now share how I have felt due to having mild depression in the past. **NOTE:** There are some types of depression that are very severe, like thoughts of committing suicide, hurting yourself and violent behavior. I have never experienced any of these, so I cannot comment on feelings I have never felt. **NOTE:** Please if you are experiencing any of the above feelings or maybe something different from them you should seek medical attention now! There are specialist in this field that can help you with severe depression. Thank you and God Bless you all.

Now I will explain the feelings I have had with mild depression, from time to time. (Examples-of -my -mild -depression)

FEELING SLUGGISH

FEELING DOWN ON MYSELF

FEELING NERVOUS

FEELING LONELY

FEELING A LOSS OF INTEREST

FEELING A LOSS OF APPETITE

FELLING STRESSED OUT
ABOUT NOTHING

These are some of the ways I would feel when I experienced mild depression. I believe we all have some type of mild depression from time to time. When I started felling the warning signs of depression coming on I make myself get out of the house or talk on the phone or maybe go for a drive. The thing is that you must force yourself to do something. Learn to smile and think good thoughts , when you start to notice these feelings coming on you have began to identify with them, so don't sit around getting more depressed, do something to help snap yourself out of it. Let yourself be in control (Don't let depression rule over you). I know sometimes it's not so easy to do, but as you start taking control you should be able to handle it much better over time. Here is a testimonial of one of my friends that has experienced extreme depression over time to help give you some insight on how depression can affect some people. He asked if he could share this bit of information with you, he is not a counselor or a doctor of any kind, just a simple hard working family man that cares for others well being.

HIS STORY

Hi folks, my name is A J and from the start of my teenage years I have had problems with depression. I do feel that my low self esteem contributed to my depression and soon it quickly turned to anger and sometimes a feeling of hate! I found myself not wanting to be around other people at times. I also lost interest in almost everything. I even started to slowly starve myself. I would stay to myself and would not even talk to anyone and barely even my family. I felt so alone and hopeless most of the time and no one could understand what I was going through. Including myself at times. Now some years down the road as I have grown older, I now find that it is hard just keeping it at bay. Not long ago I had major surgery that went terribly wrong.

So after going to see countless doctors and trying to find one that would fix me, which I haven't yet (It seems like doctors today, just won't take a stand and admit that another doctor really messed up! What a damn shame! What happened to the doctors oath?) Since then I have slipped into a deep dark depression once again. It was without a doubt driven by anger towards the doctor that screwed me up! I started feeling like there was no hope for me. No matter what doctor I went to see they told me they just could not fix my botched up mess!

My world just seemed to close in again, but luckily in this day in age in my life I have a very loving wife and two wonderful children that I love so very much. As my depression grew stronger each day I started isolating myself from them. I would spend hours out on the back porch or somewhere outside. I no longer wanted to do any family activities with them at all. I didn't want to leave the house to go to their school plays, pick them up from school, or go to any sports games that they might have been playing either. (And I dearly love my kids) When I would try to sleep, I would have the most awful nightmares. I then slowly pulled away from reality even more.

When my kids would come to me to give them a kiss goodnight, I would just push them away and sometimes yell at them! I would tell them to leave me the hell alone. I then fell even deeper as a few weeks had past. I was smoking 5 packs of cigarettes a day. I got to the point where I could not sleep and when I did sleep it was only for a few hours a week. I stopped eating and taking showers, I did not care about anything or anyone anymore. What is so sad is that my wife asked me if she needed to take the kids and leave for awhile. Man when I heard her say that I really hit rock bottom! I felt that I got to the point where I did not care about her or the kids. I had told her she would be better off without me, to please leave me alone. She asked me what will we do with out you, we love you honey? I simply told her I just don't care! Folks at that point in my deep depression and my state of mind, I really did not care. When I realized I might lose my family over something I just couldn't control, I decided I would just end it all and take my life (How sad). I just did not want to suffer and I could not stand for my family to see me like this. I have had enough,

I proclaimed. So later on that night, I went from room to room and kissed my kids as they were sleeping and told them that I was sorry and that I loved them very much. Then as I walked down the hallway to my bedroom where my wife was sleeping, I stopped for a few minutes just to listen to her breath for what would be the last time. I leaned over and I kissed her forehead and told her that I loved her so very much, and that I'm sorry for what I'm about to do and please forgive me. As she lie there sleeping I told her that I would never forget hoe she completed my life and I would watch over her and the kids if the lord forgives me and lets me into heaven. At that moment a tear fell from my eye and fell on her face, I walked out of our bedroom and went to the kitchen where she kept all the medications.

I went through them all until I found the strongest . I opened the pill bottle and emptied them in my mouth. I then washed them down with a bottle of Mr. Clean. I began to pray that the lord Jesus Christ would end my pain, mentally and physically. To please forgive me for leaving my family this way. I then went and sat down on the living room floor and waited for that bright white light that I had heard about from those that had seen it. I began to feel weightless and as I was floating out of my body I knew this was it. That was the last thing I remember and surprisingly I woke up the next morning, confused and mad! The only thought in my head was that I should have died. I told my wife about a week later that I had tried to take my own life.

I don't think she believed me or maybe she didn't want to think that I was really at the point of taking my own life. She was scared and did not know how to help me. As time went on and with some counseling I'm doing well and life is great. I'm sure glad the lord had mercy on me and let me live to enjoy another day praising him and spending time with my wife and kids. You know it is very easy to slide right back in a state of severe depression. I really have to watch myself from time to time. I rely on my family and friends. From time to time they might say, "You seem to be feeling down today or is there something weighing on your mind?" They ask if I would like to talk about it and you know that talking about things before they get to bad can really help. So if you need to talk to someone choose your spouse, a family member, or just some good ole counseling.

Please do what I failed to do and get some help at the start of it all. God Bless. Thank you for letting me share my story with you, that's what life is about helping each other. Hey, keep on smiling through the years. This experience inspired me to write a song, that I hope in the future everyone will enjoy. It's called I got one more day so here I go again. Thank you my loving savior.

The bible says in PSALM 9:9 "The lord is a refuge for the oppressed, A stronghold in the times of trouble." PSALM 28:2 "Hear my cry for mercy as I call to you for help, as I lift up my hands toward your most holy place.

DON'T APOLOGIZE

Apologize? I don't think so! Would a diabetic or a person with cancer or any type of illness or disorder apologize? I would hope not, we cannot help it if we were born with something wrong or have been diagnosed with a medical Condition. Listen, if you have some type of these disorders and someone close to you at home or work asks you to apologize when your behavior seems less than worthy or appealing or maybe embarrassing to them. I believe I would have to take a long look and ask myself if I should be with this person or work along side of this prideful, arrogant, into themselves person. Talk about no compassion! Folks this is why the chapter TELL THEM ABOUT IT, IS IN THE BOOK. Apply it right away.

Now before you get all bent out of shape at someone over nothing, ask yourself is this my fault? Have you even told them how you feel sometimes and what is wrong with you? For example: Awhile back I was out with my dog trainer, Ron and we were working on an underground dog wire fence and I mentioned I was writing this book on anxiety/panic disorders. He asked, what made you want to do that? I told him that I was diagnosed with these types of disorders, I had fought back and came up with a few techniques of my own that has helped me and others. He then looked up from the ground where he was digging and said, "Man, awhile back I had some of that anxiety over worrying about a few things." You see, after all this time I thought he knew about my disorders.

I had mentioned them before to him, but maybe he didn't understand me. See this was my fault. Now he knows and he surely knows what it feels like to have anxiety from time to time. So folks don't ever apologize for something like a medical condition that you may have.

God Bless you and keep you.

The bible says in PSALM 34:2 "My soul will boast in the lord, let the afflicted hear and rejoice."

TEST PAGE

TEST YOURSELF TO SEE WHAT YOU HAVE LEARNED

_____

_____

_____

_____

_____

_____

_____

_____

_____

_____

_____

_____

_____

_____

_____

_____

_____

_____

_____

_____

_____

_____

_____

BE THANKFUL FOR
THE GOOD DAYS

This is a chapter that you will probably want to come back several times in the future as you begin to identify and hog tie one or more of these disorders you may suffer from. For example: Like me, I will do great most of the time and then I would notice the nervousness coming on and now with identifying with it for some time I know how my mind will react. It may bother me for 2-3 days or more. As I look back on the month or months that I have felt fine, I then thank god for all the good days I've had. Believe me It beats the heck out of the days in the beginning when I was diagnosed. That was terrible my friends. Sometimes I will feel anxious or overwhelming fear due to a social phobia, I feel weird around crowds, in large stores or meeting someone new. I bet you feel this way too sometimes?

Folks at the start of your battle with these disorders be thankful for just one good day and know that there is many more to follow. I did it with my way of thinking and you can too. The human mind is so powerful and we only use just a small part of it, we have to learn to use more of it to gain more knowledge about things we don't know much about. Look at it this way, use creative thinking. Now take a few moments to think about something you know nothing about at all. Well have you thought of something? Now how much do you really know about the product or thing you thought of? I bet very little or nothing! If this is the case how can you acquire some knowledge about it? You could read books, go to college or a trade school, etc.

I said that to say this, it's the same way with these disorders. Not until you get some knowledge about them, how in the world can you start to learn how they may affect your mind or body? In my first weeks of suffering through the fear, pain, and complete aggravation of these disorders, you can bet I would have given my last dollar for it to go away, but I soon figured out that was not going to happen. For me personally, I have never found or have I heard of a quick fix for these disorders. Folks, knowledge is power and it will take you down the road to recovering from most or all the effects of these disorders.

Now my brother in law used to suffer from panic attacks and as we talked on the phone a few days ago he told me he has not had one in a long time. He considered it a blessing from the lord. (I do believe in the healing power of god) So if there are days when you feel down, anxious, or fearful just pray and let it take it's course, and soon you will begin to identify with the effects it has on you. As you begin taking control and facing them head on they will seem to grow weaker and weaker each day, week, and month. You will be thankful for the good days and this chapter you can refer back on to help keep your chin up off the ground. You maybe saying, hey that's easier said than done! Well so is saying "I Love You" how many people say this each day to someone and really mean it, or has it become easier for them to say it? Have they forgot the actions that go along with saying these words? So start today by speaking to these disorders like this,

I will learn and take control, I will crush you like a mighty flood. I am strong, a fighter and I won't be ran out of town on a rail. I am an over comer through Jesus Christ. So quit being a big baby stand up and put on your boxing gloves, and speak firmly to these disorders. Tell them that each time you hit me I will you back twice as hard! Now the hitting back is the knowledge that you've learned each time. You will grow stronger and wiser in the days to come, I did. Soon you will have more and more good days as you push on and you will be so thankful for the good days you have had. Remember don't think negative or keep yourself clammed up in the house all day get out and get on with your life just the way I did. Soon you will be able to "Identify It and Hog Tie It". God Bless you on your great days ahead.

The bible says in PROVERBS 2:6 "For the lord gives wisdom and from his mouth knowledge and understanding."

The bible says in PROVERBS 1:5 "A wise man will listen and increase his learning, and a discerning man will obtain guidance."

TEST PAGE

TEST YOURSELF TO SEE WHAT
YOU HAVE LEARNED

_____

_____

_____

_____

_____

_____

_____

_____

_____

_____

_____

_____

_____

_____

_____

_____

_____

_____

_____

_____

_____

_____

ALCOHOL/DRUGS/
NATURAL HERBS ETC.

So you have anxiety disorder and depression and want to consume excessive amounts of alcohol. Well consider this, Too much alcohol is bad for your health and has been known to cause depression and intensify the effects of anxiety. See it's like this, when you have anxiety sometimes it is hard to relax and get free of that nervous feeling that just eats at you, not to mention "Insomnia". Some people fall into this little trap the same way I did. It's called self medicating. I would start with a couple of beers before I went to bed and this would take some of the edge off of me. Then I would have a couple more until I was consuming a few beers a night. It felt good at the time just to get some rest, but soon I felt more depressed and run down over time. If you have fallen into this trap, please stop now!

It will only lead to more destruction with your disorders. It's a shame that there are so many people out there that are depressed and have different types of disorders that constantly self medicate themselves. Some use alcohol and others may use some type of drugs that they may be abusing. They feel happy and cheerful while they are somewhat stoned, but the next morning they just seem to crash once again. So if you are doing this, please stop and get some help or just say no more self medicating for me. Don't use this as a crutch! Learn to identify with how anxiety affects you and you will grow stronger and less afraid of it over time. If you keep self medicating you will never be able to deal with how anxiety affects you Be Strong! Become a fighter and knock anxiety out cold. Don't lay down like a big baby and take it.

Yes, I know that lack of sleep and feeling nervous is so overwhelming at times. Just remember that as you begin to identify with the signs of these disorders you will soon be able to get a handle on it and your body will come back to somewhat a normal state just the way mine did. Be patient it will take a little time. You could talk to your doctor about this issue like I did. He gave me a small generic dose of Zanax and some sleeping pills, I used only one sleeping pill. After a few months time of taking Zanax that was a thirty day supply, now lasts two and a half months. Don't make these medicines be your crutch. You should not drink alcohol with these types of medications, because it can intensify the effects. It says on the bottle no alcohol!

Read about all medicines you may be going to take. For Example: I was prescribed prevacid for reflux disease and after a few days of taking it I felt weird. I later figured out it was throwing me into panic attacks again. Evidently, it has some type of chemical that relates to other types of medicines I could not take before like paxil, and lexapro etc. So know what your taking . Read about them and ask your doctor questions. It's your health!

NATURAL, VITAMINS, HERBS & TEA

I did find that some of these products worked for me. Like Chamomile Tea, (The calming and relaxing blend). This worked well along with some local honey mixed in. It did calm me down some and helped me to relax before I went to bed, very tasty and soothing. A friend of mine that does not have this disorder, but does experience trouble sleeping, along with stress also. She takes Melotonin 300 mcg to help her sleep and she just lives by it. So she said I should try this it may work for you too, I did and "BAM" it worked! I was so excited. Now see here is a natural type of sleeping formula we can use. NOTE: Before you take anything natural please check with your doctor to make sure it will not affect your current medications, or your health due to different types of health problems you may already have. Just be safe it's your body. So control what goes in it.

I found out early on one of the things that may cause this chemical imbalance is low Serotonin in our brain so I have searched for something natural that can add Serotonin and I came up with some. Amino Acids help in the regulation of our brain chemicals, it helps our brain with Serotonin and neurotransmitters. Amino Acids are known to be safer than prescription drugs. Do not take more than the normal dose listed on the bottle unless directed by your health care provider. Amino Acids have also been said to help with depression. Kava has also been known to help with depression, anxiety, and insomnia. Vitamin B is great for leg cramps and they play a role in helping brain and nerve function. Sometimes insomnia and anxiety can be caused by Universal Muscle Tension. You might want to try calcium and magnesium for this. There are vegetables that have higher amounts of Serotonin in them. I have been told.

After some research on my own, I found that Broccoli is to be one of them. I'm sure there are more out there, just ask someone. You know your body better than anyone, so do some research of your own and you are sure to make the right decision. God Bless you and great health in the future. "(WARNING)" Never use any kind of illegal drugs, this would be a fatal mistake! Please educate your children about all types of drugs and what they can do to them, others and their families. Illegal drug use has destroyed many good families and lives. Please say no to drugs. Thank You for your courage to stand against illegal drug use. FOOD FOR THOUGHT: One night a father overheard his son praying, "Dear God, make me the kind of man my daddy is". Later that night, the father prayed, "Dear God, make me the kind of man my son wants me to be". (Take some time today and pray together as a family) God Bless You.

God truly does love you, so smile at someone today and let them see the love of Jesus shining through you. Pray for others as they pray for you.

TEST PAGE

TEST YOURSELF TO SEE WHAT
YOU HAVE LEARNED

_____

_____

_____

_____

_____

_____

_____

_____

_____

_____

_____

_____

_____

_____

_____

_____

_____

_____

_____

_____

_____

FREEDOM FROM ADDICTIONS

Well it has been said by a lot of medical researchers over the years that in 22 to 30 days you can break a bad habit or some type of addiction. This probably does work for those of us that are obedient and really set our mind to it. There are several types of habits and addictions such as-

Cigarettes

Chewing Tobacco

Alcohol

Gambling

Chocolate

Sex

Prescribed Drugs/Man-Made Illegal Drugs

Food

Work

Clothes/Shoes Etc.

So see we all have addictions that can come between our real responsibilities that we should be taking care of. Example: Our bodies, if we choose to use tobacco or consume large amounts of alcohol or food as well, we can harm our bodies.

If we choose to gamble or spend a lot of money we don't have on clothes and shoes etc. This will certainly cause us to neglect our financial responsibilities and before we know it were in deep debt and in trouble. (Don't rob Peter to pay Paul). Sexual Addiction: Yes, sex can be an addiction as well! Believe it or not there has been a lot of good marriages go down the drain due to infidelity. A lot of the time this addiction starts by he or she, married or not, purchasing pornography in some form or another. This then leads to sexual perversion, in many different ways. I have seen people fall into this trap many times and it is a hard addiction to break! Work: Some of us are really addicted to our work. We enjoy it and it becomes like a hobby to us, but how does this affect the other people in our lives? They may feel neglected or jealous. Is work taking precious time away from the people you love the most? Just learn to take some time to relax!

Prescription Drugs: Sometimes due to surgery or chronic pain we all may be prescribed some type of addicting drug. You should take them as directed by your doctor or this can turn into a living nightmare. Sometimes this leads to people becoming addicted to feel good drugs as I call them. The trouble starts when they cannot get another prescription from that doctor so they choose another doctor to get more. Then when that well runs dry they start buying them from people they know and when that well runs dry they start faking prescriptions or buying them sometimes off the street. If their money bag goes dry then they sometimes result to stealing money or some other immoral behavior just to get a fix. Illegal Drugs: Man what a problem! I've seen illegal drugs just take people and their families and just tear them apart and ravage their lives. Their job falls to pieces, their family, their children suffer, their health deteriorates and so on. This is a no win situation! So please don't destroy your life and the people you love. If you feel you have a problem just talk to someone about it now.

God Bless You for having the courage to get some help.

Now we all know that different types or addictions are much harder to break than others. I remember what a close friend of mine told me one time, after I told him about a friend of mine that was an alcoholic for years and kept getting thrown in jail for public drunkiness and DUI's over several years. I asked him one day why don't you just quit? A few times he would go to AA meetings and it did him no good. He also had to spend time in prison still this did him no good. Then my friend told me he was a recovering alcoholic and had been sober for years. He said something that made a lot of sense. He said, anyone that has an addiction has to want help before they will ever get any better. Just like gambling, move away from the temptation or food, just quit buying addicting foods. For shopping, set up a budget for yourself and stay with it! For the abuse of drugs of any kind, just do yourself and others a favor and don't get started taking medicines that are so addicting.

I bet your saying to yourself right now, what does this have to do with anxiety/panic disorder? Well lets take a look. I take a mild dosage of Zanax for nerves sometimes (Only when I need It). See if we depend on it all the time it just becomes a crutch. Just like other drugs, gambling or excessive shopping. It all causes stress and destruction in some way or another to you and your loved ones. The point is that if we reduce stress in our lives, we can deal with and identify with our disorders in a much quicker time frame. You will be on your way to conquering these disorders. God Bless You and good health.

The bible says in MATTHEW 19:18 "Which one? The man inquired? Jesus replied, Do not murder, commit adultery, steal, give false testimony, honor your father and mother and love your neighbor as yourself".

The bible says in 1 JOHN 2:16 "For everything in the world , the cravings of sinful man, the lust of his eyes and the boasting of what he has and does comes not from the father, but from the world". So jump into the word of God and let Jesus help you out. God Bless You on your journey to freedom.

TEST PAGE

TEST YOURSELF TO SEE WHAT
YOU HAVE LEARNED

_____

_____

_____

_____

_____

_____

_____

_____

_____

_____

_____

_____

_____

_____

_____

_____

_____

_____

_____

_____

_____

_____

_____

HEALTHY DIET AND EXERCISE

Folks if you have anxiety disorder or panic attacks you need to know that being tired and not eating properly, especially the wrong kinds of foods can make you feel tired and worn down. This can result in you feeling edgy and you may develop higher amounts of stress in your day. I know that it did in me. Just sitting around feeling tired all the time can make us feel lazy. We seem to lose our drive for things we want to do or should be doing. It affects our performance at work or at home and sometimes makes us just a procrastinator. You should exercise as often as you can to help keep your stress level down. NOTE: If you have other health problems or you are on certain types of medications that may affect your ability to get some exercise, please check with your doctor first so that he or she can recommend what you should or should not do. For Example: Don't just jump on a treadmill and take off walking or running unless you have a personal trainer or your doctor first.

There have been many of people do this and ended up in the Emergency Room. The same way with foods, how will they affect your medications and your health? Now my mother has to be careful of what type of food she eats, because she is in kidney failure. So if you have medical conditions you should discuss exercise and foods with your doctor. Quit eating out all the time, it's just not good for you. There are so many chemicals and additives in fast food today and that is why we are getting fatter and fatter. Plus there is not much nutrition value there either. Start making your own food at home at least you know what is in it! When I started to exercise I chose a low impact workout. I used five pound weights I bought at Wal-Mart and some push up pads.

I began to slowly walk, as well as some bending and stretching exercises. Just start out slowly. As for eating, look for healthy recipes that will give you strength and vitality. It's so important to get the right amount of sleep. To help you not to get so worn down as you cruise through your day. So take it from me, exercise, eat right and live a stress free life. You will find out soon just how much better your problems with having anxiety will get. God Bless You on your journey to a better life..

The bible says in PSALM 32:8 "I will point

out the road that you should follow, I will be your teacher and watch over you".

Just a thought: There is no better exercise for strengthening the heart than reaching down and lifting someone up.

TEST PAGE

TEST YOURSELF TO SEE WHAT YOU HAVE LEARNED

_____

_____

_____

_____

_____

_____

_____

_____

_____

_____

_____

_____

_____

_____

_____

_____

_____

_____

_____

_____

_____

THE KISS FACTOR

I bet for all of you that has never heard this said before and now you're just itching to know what it means. This funny phrase was told to me by a good friend of mine, years ago. I laughed and said just what does that mean? So he explained it to me and it has been the way that I have lived my life for years. It means (Keep-It-Simple-Stupid). Now it takes me back to when I would jump the gun and try to set an idea in motion without thinking it through first. I would just take off on a whim and get way ahead of where I should have started in the first place. I should have started from the basics, just a simple approach. I just failed to start with the "Kiss Factor". You know, if you think about the kiss factor, that's basically where it all started for all of us. When we were born, we had nothing. Man wasn't life simple then?

We had to crawl before we could walk, and walk before we could run. Folks the kiss factor is not to imply that any one of us is stupid, but you have to admit we all have done some pretty stupid things in the past. I know I have and Thank god I am forgiven. Now when I was talking about crawling, walking, and running you can compare these to the disorders you maybe encountering. So think about this, If you have hope you can begin to crawl and if you gain some knowledge you can began to walk. When you begin to start to identify with the effects that anxiety or panic disorder has on you, then you can run. These are examples of how you can grow and put some distance between you and the effects of these disorders.

Yes, I do know that anxiety and panic attacks can cause us great fear and grip us like a vise! Well, If you would run to them instead of running away from them, you will soon become more familiar with them and have less fear. Take control. I know that you are scared now, but look at me and others that overcome the fear of these disorders. Knowledge is power. Just began to think back as far as you can when you were a child. Try to find out if there was maybe something traumatic that happened to you or someone you loved.

I did this a lot I would lay awake and think and one night I figured it out. It was the death of my father. Years ago I was helping my dad finish up his work and after a little while he said, I am sweating and I don't feel so well. I told him to go on home or I could take him to the hospital, but as he got into the truck to go home he just passed out in the seat. I freaked out! I took him out of the truck and started CPR, because the way he was breathing told me he was having a heart attack. I was in shock, but luckily there was a lady across the street that was a heart nurse and she called 911 and began to help me out. Thank God for caring people. The ambulance arrived and I can't remember much after that. They told me I was in shock.

A short time later they told me my dad had passed away. (I Love you dad and God Bless you for being a Christian man). At that time my mother was so upset and lost, my little brother and sister were still fairly young. I knew I had to be there for all of them and at the same time my son was only a year old and I was getting a divorce. Talk about emotional stress! After things got somewhat settled down, I just drifted away from reality for about two years or so. I began to drink and frequent the bars. I lived a very ungodly life style. Before all this happened I went to the same church for years and served God. After all this trauma I drifted away from God. I left him in the tough times, but thank God he never left me. Thank You Jesus.

I became distant from my family and I was hard and bitter too. Was I mad at God for taking my dad, my best friend? Probably in some way. I think for a lot of years I just put this traumatic event in the back of my mind. I felt so overwhelmed at the time, I just could not handle it. I also learned I never took the time to grieve over the death of my father. So one day I took some time and just let it all out. Man that felt great. I believe it started a healing process in my soul. Folks there are things that get deep rooted in our minds, that we need to face. Want to face yours today? Take yourself back to the simpler side of life.

There may be things that is in your past that are hard to face and you should work on ways to talk about and deal with them. Just forgive yourself and forgive others. Have you got to know you lately? Spend some time with yourself, you may just figure out that you really love yourself. I believe that if you come to terms and truly love yourself, you will find out just how easy it is to forgive and love others. When I took a trip down memory lane time and time again, I noticed something about myself as well. I remembered that when I would go to school, I would sit at the back of the class or to the side.

I did not want to be in a crowd and I always

seemed to need a quick exit. I still do the same thing at a concert, movie and at church I will not sit in a crowd. I would feel nervous or before a meeting or before I would perform in a music event. Then It hit me, I probably had anxiety all my life, along with a social disorder too. I believe that when I became a little older and my life settled down, It came rushing in like a flood. Just a quick reminder: If you have a panic attack, you will probably think you are having a heart attack, most of us feel that way at first. You will go to the Emergency Room and get checked out, just to find that you had a panic attack. Please follow up and make sure there is nothing seriously wrong with you.

If all is good, don't get caught up in the medical test nightmare like I did. It cost me thousands of dollars. Your mind keeps on telling you there is something else wrong. Like, I think I have a brain tumor or it's my gallbladder etc. If you have been checked out by your doctor and everything is fine then don't fall for these mind playing tricks. It will fade away a little at a time, just be patient. My dad told me one time, that to hate someone is a full time job, but to love someone is effortless. The bible says in REVELATION 4:11 "You are worthy, our Lord and God, to receive glory, honor and power, for you created all things and by your will they were created and have their being" Praise the Lord for he is worthy of our praise. We are over comers through Jesus Christ. God Bless.

TEST PAGE

TEST YOURSELF TO SEE WHAT
YOU HAVE LEARNED

_____

_____

_____

_____

_____

_____

_____

_____

_____

_____

_____

_____

_____

_____

_____

_____

_____

_____

_____

_____

_____

_____

_____

E BAY SAVED THE DAY

Now, after my diagnosis I found that I didn't want to leave the house much or be around a lot of people and I felt extremely nervous when I would venture out and drive. Well one night I was bored and I remember someone talking about an auction site called E Bay. I did not know anything about E Bay or how to set it up, because at the time I was not computer savvy. I looked it up and then followed the easy steps to become a member so that I might learn how to sell things on it's auction site. Well it worked and then I set up my pay pal account, and this was somewhat easy as well, but I had to drive all the way to my bank to retrieve the 3 or 4 digit pin number so that I could finish my pay pal account.

This might not seem like a big step to you, but when you live as far out from town as I do, It forced me to drive to take care of something important. It also made me have to go into the bank and talk to with others. At that time it wasn't easy to do because of the social phobia I was dealing with. I then had my E Bay account set up and ready to learn how to sell my items. After figuring out that I would have to find things to sell, I started digging through closets and my storage sheds. I found so many things I had not used in years. I then spent time cleaning them up and then I had to take pictures of all my items to display them on E Bay.

So once again I was forced out of the house to go back to town and shop for a reasonable digital camera and a tripod stand, this was fun and took my mind off this depressing disorder for awhile. I then learned how to upload my pictures on the site and with dial up this was making me a patient man. That was good because it wasted away those idle hours and kept my mind on my new venture. I soon noticed I was feeling much better. I had figured out how to slip away from a lot of fear I was having and I felt that I was achieving something each day.

It was so hard to work my existing business because of having to deal directly with my customers face to face. This little venture became exciting in the days and months that passed. I felt that every morning I got up I had a purpose and felt that I had an in home cash machine, It was so exciting to go to my auction site and see what the bids were on my products. All this so called junk I had laying around paid my bills each month. My bills weren't that much, I'm debt free and I was learning a new business venture. God provided a way for me even in my toughest times. Thank You Lord. What helped me the most in this venture was when I sold a product, I would have to pack it up safely and take it to the Post Office and mail it off. I also would have to weigh it and compute the shipping charges.

I could have had Fed Ex or UPS stop by , but that would just be another crutch I could lean on. I used this little business as a form of my therapy to help me get out of the house and get around people and to also help me get back to overcoming the fear of driving. Sometimes it was a struggle just to drive to town. I would have to pull over due to a panicky feeling, so when this would happen I would get off the road a safe distance or pull into a parking lot so that another car would not run over me. (Remember as you protect yourself, please protect other drivers as well. Always use caution while driving and extra caution if your having a panic attack). Well, after awhile of selling on E Bay my friends would ask me to list some of their things and that was fun.

It was like winning the lottery. A friend of mine said he had a bunch of old stuff in his garage and we went through it and found some neat stuff that he was going to through away. Well I brought it home and put it on the site and sold it. He made some extra cash too, he was excited. I am helping myself and others. Now this is funny, he found a little paper box in some junk and told me about it. I said, don't throw that away let me see it. I looked at the box and it measured 1 ½" deep and 2 ½ inches wide and had a paper label on it that read Remington Clean Bore Bullets. So I listed it on E Bay and in about an hour it was up to $56.00 and then a little while later it climbed to $70.00.

The next day it topped out at $117.00 what a little treasure. They say one mans junk is another mans treasure, I guess that's true. This little venture turned out to be a lot of fun for me and gave me some pretty good therapy as well. Now you may be saying what does this have to do with anxiety/panic/social disorders? Well, It is so important to keep yourself busy and keep your mind off the nervousness and to help keep you from getting more depressed. Little ventures like this, as well as hobbies gives us pleasure and hope on not feeling completely useless. Maybe you want to start a little venture or learn to play an instrument, begin to read and study the whole bible, maybe write a song or just write a book.

I know that you will find something that gives

you happiness. This will help you push yourself into something you enjoy and put some distance between you and these disorders, so that you can begin to identify with how they are affecting you each day. God Bless You for taking a stand and not just lying down and taking all the abuse that these disorders try to dish out. I believe that if you plan to climb a mountain you are going to have to start at the bottom and work your way up. Look at these disorders the same way. It might take some time, but eventually you will reach the top and then you can rejoice, because now you have conquered this huge mountain that once taunted you. Start climbing the mountain that stands in your way and soon you will reach the top, be patient this will take some time. The bible says in EXODUS 20:9-10 "You are to labor for six days and do all the work, but the seventh day is a Sabbath to the Lord your God".

(Worry is interest paid on trouble before it is due) God Bless You and great health and happiness.

TEST PAGE

TEST YOURSELF TO SEE WHAT
YOU HAVE LEARNED

_____

_____

_____

_____

_____

_____

_____

_____

_____

_____

_____

_____

_____

_____

_____

_____

_____

_____

_____

_____

BECOME A GIVER

Be a giver why? It just fells dogone good to help others that are in need. I have always been a person that loved to give and help folks out, just the way my parents did. If they heard someone was in need of groceries, money or a ride to work they would reach out to help them. Not for their own gain, but they just had a passion for man kind. God said be a cheerful giver and you shouldn't boast about your giving. Through the years I have always been a man that would give of my time or money. There were a few years that I kind of got off on the wrong track when I drifted away from God and lived a more worldly life style. That is when I stopped giving as much as I did.

I seemed to have less compassion for my fellow man. I now ask myself was it because I was struggling or had I just become somewhat bitter towards others? Could it have to do with my fathers death or my divorce? For a long time I did struggle due to irresponsibility, but it wasn't anyone's fault, but mine. The only one I could blame was me! The word of god says we should be a good steward of our finances and for me I could not hold onto one single cent. This was due to my wild and crazy life style. I believe first of all it was because of drifting away from God and doing things the way I wanted to do them. (Wow! How is that working for me?). I do feel after my dad's unexpected death and a sad divorce I fell into a state of depression.

I felt sad and lonely most of the time. This went on for a few years, until one day I was out splitting wood in the winter sleet, I had been feeling down lately and asking myself why go on? What is the meaning of life? When I had thought about everything I had done over those past few years, I noticed that there were very few that had anything to do with serving god or giving to others. I had become bitter and it was all about me. Then I started thinking back to what I was taught as a kid by my parents and at church. I had accepted Jesus as my lord and savior when I was quite young and for several years I attended the same church and realized that man what a great and blessed life I had.

I gave up on God in my tough times, but he didn't give up on me. On that very day out splitting wood I looked up and said, God is there any way you could help me or my life is over? I have hit rock bottom and in that moment I felt the love of Jesus just surround me. I knew that there was still room at the foot of the cross for me. Thank You Jesus. I felt the lord speak to me through my spirit and he said, "I will make you a new creature in Christ". I will set you free of this bondage that you are in. I will forgive you if you will only ask me with a true heart. I will cast your sins as far as the east is to the west, never to remember them again". This is one of the promises of Gods word. So from that day on God kept his promise to me and he gave me joy, hope, healing and happiness.

He also set me free from the bar scene that I thought I loved. My friends seemed to change slowly and new faithful friends were added. I found a great little country church awhile after that. What a great pastor we have there. God Bless You Pastor Rex for preaching the true word of God to me and others, but you know I had one more problem. It was on giving, even years ago when I attended church regularly. The little part a lot of us get hung up on (Giving our Tithes). I was always taught, we should bring our tithes into the storehouse (Church) and give 10% of what we bring in. I was like others, I just couldn't seem to let go of that 10%, I always made excuses. Like, I have to pay my rent, my electric is due or maybe it was something else I wanted for myself.

After God had mercy on my life this last time I asked for his help, I learned a great lesson. Would you like to know what it was? It was that without god in my life I just could not survive! I tried it and I failed again and again. See he created us and everything we have belongs to him anyway. Now you might be asking why pay to go to church? Your not, you are being obedient to gods word. Put your faith in god and I promise he will bless you beyond every means. That's what he has done in my life. I'm a living example of his mercy and wonderful grace. Here is what I have done and you can do the same. I took out some paper and started my own prayer list and would pray for whoever was on my list.

The funny thing is that there are a lot of folks that don't even know that I have been praying for them. Hey, don't forget to put yourself on there as well. Over the past few years I have seen some miracles and things take place that were such a blessing to me. What a change he has made in my life giving me love, peace and joy. No more bitterness, God said he would make me a new creature in Christ and he did. Thank You Jesus for your faithfulness, Amen. Friend spend time in prayer, God really does care and he loves us so much.

Now let's go back to the part about giving tithes and lending a hand to others in need. I made out a notebook log to keep track of where I gave my tithe money to each week or month. I made this log long before I made a prayer list log. On this log I would put dates out to one side and then name of one of my jobs, a car I may have sold or a blessing from someone else to me. I would then times that by the amount I received times 10% and that would be my tithe. Also, I gave things away like a car, food or bought someone's bible etc. Sometimes I would increase my giving. (Man it sure feels good to give). I would help folks with cancer or give to hospitals to help kids with cancer, CBN to help drill water wells in different countries and to help folks that had lost their jobs or about to lose their homes. Oh and of course my church home.

When I look at that tithe book sometimes It is amazing how much God has trusted me with over the years. It was always said to me "You just can't out give God"! One day awhile back as I sat in my office chair looking at this log book a tear came to my eye. He has truly blessed me to bless others and you can't out give God there is just no way. He promised he would pour out his blessings on me and he surely has kept his word. He hasn't left this seed begging for bread! I am truly blessed beyond every means each day. Friends, today trust god at his word and become a cheerful giver. Now you might be saying, what does this have to do with Anxiety/Panic/Social Phobia Disorders?

Well lets get this question hammered out. In believing and trusting God and following his word, along with spending time in prayer for others as well as becoming obedient to Gods word on giving. This promotes a much better and positive attitude, reduces stress in your life and gives you the chance to help others. If you will begin to make some changes in your Christian walk with God and pray for others, God will begin to open up doors in your life you never expected to open. Take it from me, been there, done that, even when I was serving the lord I went through the deep dark valley of fighting depression, anxiety, panic attacks and a social phobia. Look folks sometimes we don't know why we have to go through the tough times in our lives, maybe it's a learning experience to test our faith or to help others get through things they are going through.

God says I will not leave you nor forsake you. As I went through my fight with these disorders I did not leave my walk with Jesus. You just got to praise the lord in the good times as well as the bad. Just to let you know, my outcome is great! We surely do serve a healing God, I'm a prime example of that today. God Bless You all on your journey to serving God and becoming a cheerful giver. The bible says in 2 CORINTHIANS 9:7 "Each man should give what he has decided in his heart to give, not reluctantly or under compulsion, for God loves a cheerful giver". The bible says in PROVERBS 3:9 "Honor the lord with your wealth, with the first fruits of all your crops". PROVERBS 3:10 says, "Then your barns will be filled to overflowing, and your vats will brim over with new wine". Thank God for the blessings he bestows on you today.

TEST PAGE

TEST YOURSELF TO SEE WHAT
YOU HAVE LEARNED

THE WINDOW AND THE WORLD

There's a whole world out here just waiting on you, come join us. Lately have you felt that your stuck in your own little world? You just don't know how to move forward. Well consider this, lets say you have grown to a point where all you do is keep yourself shut up in your home or office. So take a minute and walk to a window, open the curtain or blind, well what do you see? I know sometimes we feel scared to journey out into the great outdoors, well today take a stand and make yourself get out more and more. You will find that when you quit hiding in a small dark place, you may just get excited and you will feel much better each time you venture outside.

If you are fighting depression or anxiety it is so important to get out and find something to do each day. There are so many people today that spend so much of their time indoors that they forgot about the things they used to enjoy. Shut off the TV, computer, or video games and drag out the charcoal grill and some lawn chairs and have a cookout. Go to a park, walk around and listen to the sounds of nature. I know there is something in this big ole world of ours you must love doing. Don't let depression and anxiety scare you or control you. Start enjoying the things you really love and soon you will find that the signs of depression and anxiety will start to fade away, because now you have become excited and have decided to go and be apart of a whole world with a million things you love to do.

All you have to do is pick something you love to do and go with it. So, are you sitting around all the time worrying or shut up in a dark room, maybe your pacing the floor scared of bill collectors? Then, once in a while you look out a window and say to yourself, there's that drab and dreary world again! Yet at the same time the world is looking back at you saying, come out it's ok come join in on the fun. You must push yourself along. Get excited about meeting new people or a new hobby.

Why do you think that elderly people have such a hard time not getting depressed or over anxious in their older age? It's because they have been used to working or gardening or some type of hobby. As they grow older and less able to do the things that they so love. Sometimes they get depressed or have anxiety, especially if they are unable to get out and do the things they want to do. That is why we have senior citizens hall and trips etc. These places give them a hope and a reason to get out and look forward to each and every one of them. God Bless You Seniors. Why do we hear stories about people retiring and in a few months some of them just pass away. Most of them didn't want to retire, but they had to or was forced to, they seem to just lose the will to live, how sad.

So "I'm still young and healthy" what's your problem? Do you really just want to sit around and take the abuse that depression or anxiety can dish out to you? Or will you just grow old and never enjoy your life until one day you say I've had enough! My friend will you be to old to do the things you really want to do? Folks don't let life pass you by, start today by saying, "I will enjoy my life now and I will take control of my life back. There's a whole world out there and I plan to be apart of it". Friends if all you ever do is sit around and worry about depression or anxiety, then that's what will consume your every thought. Now every time depression or anxiety attacks you, push yourself to find something to do or go somewhere around people or noise.

When you do this, you don't give depression or anxiety a chance to take over and control you anymore and soon you will be controlling it. Use your powerful mind and be a fighter! That's what I had to do. So go open the door and yell out, I welcome you world into my life!! God Bless You and keep on smiling. The bible says in PSALM 34:4 "I sought the lord and he answered me; he delivered me from all my fears".

TEST PAGE

TEST YOURSELF TO SEE WHAT
YOU HAVE LEARNED

_____

_____

_____

_____

_____

_____

_____

_____

_____

_____

_____

_____

_____

_____

_____

_____

_____

_____

_____

_____

_____

_____

BEHAVIORAL TECHNIQUES

Hey there, I hope your feeling much better, because now you have hope. Now I want to share with you some ways I have helped myself overcome the fear of being in a crowd, walking into a large store or taking a trip etc. Maybe right now your experiencing the overwhelming feeling that I once had. Do you find it hard to go shopping or be in a crowd or maybe you feel funny talking to someone you don't even know. I sure did and it was miserable! Well after months and months of suffering I did some research on the computer and found something called behavioral therapy, as I learned some more about this subject, I then realized I could do this myself without any help from a professional and not have to pay a ridiculous amount of money either.

This type of therapy helps you deal with your fears and phobias and we all have some fear of something in this great planet of ours. The best way to deal with a fear of something is to face it head on. For Example: I have always been scared of snakes, but what has helped me overcome most of that fear is that I have a friend that catches snakes and spiders and being around him and the snakes has taught me a lot about their behavior. As I gained some knowledge from him about snakes and spiders I don't fear them near as much anymore.

He showed me what snakes were poisoness and which ones aren't. He also said that snakes are more afraid of us than we are of them. (Shoot, just look at how big we are and how little they are, Wow!). Look at it this way it's the same way with a panic, anxiety or a phobia of some type. The more knowledge you acquire about them, the safer you will feel being around them or dealing with them. Working to get over the fear of things takes some time, courage and a lot of effort, but you can do it because you have (HOPE). Put yourself out there and ease into it slowly the same way I did and you will find over time that your fear of that one thing is getting weaker as your growing stronger and taking control back.

Let me explain it like this, say you get out of your car at home after a hard days work and to your surprise your new neighbor has a large dog, he begins to run up to you barking and growling as if he was going to bite you. Well how would you feel? Probably startled and scared to death!

As the neighbor comes to your rescue, he replies, Oh he won't bite he just acts that way sometimes! So now you have calmed down and you are petting the dog. Everything is fine, but you are still somewhat afraid of the dog. So the next day you come home the same thing happens again. You are once again overcome with fear and screaming for the dog to stop!

Again the neighbor comes to save you again, again and again, until you come home a few days later and get out of your car and you guessed it, here comes that dang dog again. Although this time you just walk towards him and pat him on the head because time after time he has never bitten you, he just wants to show off a little. So the more you face your fears and the closer to them you get and learn how to deal with them, the less fearful you become. It can be a little tough at first, but soon you will conquer your fears. Now I will touch on some fears and phobias some of us are dealing with For Example:

Elevators-Some people will not ride a elevator, due to the fear of a small place with no exit between floors. They are afraid the cables might break, it will stop between floors and they don't like heights or a crowd of people they know jammed in there with them. Department Stores-Some people feel an overwhelming fear when they go into a shopping center. They feel trapped inside the store the further back they go and they begin to feel shaky, sweaty and sometimes dizzy.

Not to mention the crowd of people that are around. Standing in the checkout line can be overwhelming for them if there are a lot of people in line or the cashier has messed up. You feel like you just want to run outside to safety. If this happens to you, just try your best to stay right there as long as you can. This will help you face your fears and if you are to overwhelmed just put it in B for boogie and split! You can try again later on and little by little you will notice how much better you feel when you go shopping. Oh yea, when you are in a store like that it helps to find something you are interested in to take your mind off of it.

That's what I did and it worked. Also ask someone you are close with to go shopping with you. This can make you feel safer in the beginning and have some support as you begin to try to overcome your fears. God Bless. Now some things people are afraid of. There are a lot of people that have become afraid of the simplest things. Sometimes I think it may be due to a bad experience or something in their memory as a young child. Something traumatic. Like me for example, when I was young I remember my mother having gallbladder surgery and at that time, years ago it was a serious surgery. She was in so much pain and the scar was so long, I just couldn't get that out of my mind.

It terrified me for years. Like when I would walk into a hospital, I would feel nervous and jittery and just the thought of having surgery would frighten me to death! As I became older I had to have a test ran and that was the first time I was ever put under anesthetic. I feared this (Man I was nervous as cat on a hot tin roof), but after it was over I found that I had faced one of my biggest fears ever. Now I feel more comfortable with it. It was hard to do, but I backed my ears and went through with it. I'm glad I did. It took away a lot of my fears. So face your fears head on when you can and remember to do it safely and ask someone to help you along the way if you should need it.

The more you face your fears and the closer you get to them, the faster you will lose the overall fear of that one thing. I did it and so can you, take charge today and be an over comer. God Bless You on your way to the freedom you well deserve.

Do you have a fear or phobia of -Dogs, cats, horses, cotton, paper, hospitals, public speaking, eating in front of someone, heights, fire, water, guns, medicine, surgery, airplanes, crowds, relationships, people, small places, the dark etc.? Whatever it is that you fear the most is where you want to start with behavioral therapy. Study and learn your type of fear and then make a plan of attack to find ways to overcome it. Just start slowly and soon you will be on your way to conquering that awful fear that overtakes you. Remember to always use good judgment and most of all caution. Thanks and great health.

The bible says in ROMANS 8:31 "What shall we then say to these things? If God be for us, who can be against us" NOTE: You are a winner, you are victorious through Jesus Christ. Begin to see yourself the way God sees you.

TEST PAGE

TEST YOURSELF TO SEE WHAT
YOU HAVE LEARNED

_____

_____

_____

_____

_____

_____

_____

_____

_____

_____

_____

_____

_____

_____

_____

_____

_____

_____

_____

_____

PRAYER HELPED ME

Well folks, for years I have been attending church and it has did me a lot of good. I enjoy it as well. I have a great and understanding church family, not to mention a wonderful pastor that teaches the real word of God. A Sunday school teacher that is down to earth, fun and very open about our everyday lives. Look, we are all going to make mistakes, we are human. Only Jesus is the perfect one. When I was diagnosed with anxiety order it was a big depressing blow for me to handle. I thought my life was over and that I might be a nut case. I felt so helpless at the time and very scared, but all this time I had been giving to God and serving him in the good times.

Now since everything looked dark and bleak in my life should I just give up? Not at all! I decide to serve God in the good times and in the bad times in my life not just part of the time. So for months and months I began to pray about my sickness and yes there were times that I would have been better off to just check out of this ole world, but I stayed in there and prayed for myself and others along the way. Even though I was going through one of the darkest valleys of my life, I still kept my faith in Jesus. He gives us hope through prayer, he took away so much of my fear and gave me strength to carry on. I just began to say, "The only real peace that I have dear lord is in you. You are my lord and savior. I gave my heart to you long ago and I know that you know what's best for me".

Friends, It was prayer that got me through this awful mess of sickness. Each day God just began changing my life to a better and stronger me. So spend time in prayer each day and don't give up on God in the bad times. He is still the same today as yesterday. He loves you so very much. Give God all your problems. Not just some, but all of them and watch how he will began to bless and heal you.

Friend, ask Jesus into your heart today and he will give you the hope, peace, joy and forgiveness that you so dearly need. Won't you give him praise and glory today? Sometimes I wonder if I went through this dark valley of my life so I could see how others feel with these types of disorders. If I did it was worth it in the end, because I have had great pleasure of helping others with these disorders that may have felt that life was somewhat over. God Bless them for having the courage to go on and live a normal life.

Please don't give up my friends, there is hope and healing through Jesus Christ our lord. The bible says in ROMANS 10:17 "So then faith comes by hearing and hearing by the word of God" NOTE: Faith for healing comes by hearing Gods word concerning healing. So just as you may be taking medicine two or three times a day, do the same things with the promises in the word of God regarding healing. Allow your faith to be built up! You will be amazed at the change that will take place. God Bless and great health to you.

TEST PAGE

TEST YOURSELF TO SEE WHAT YOU HAVE LEARNED

_____

_____

_____

_____

_____

_____

_____

_____

_____

_____

_____

_____

_____

_____

_____

_____

_____

_____

_____

_____

SALVATION PRAYER

HOW TO ACCEPT JESUS AS
YOUR LORD AND SAVIOR

Hi, if you don't know Jesus Christ as your lord and savior and you want Jesus to come into your heart today to be your lord and savior, I would like to share a prayer of salvation with you to lead you to Christ.

SALVATION PRAYER: Lord Jesus, I know I am a sinner and that I cannot save myself by good works. I believe that you died and shed your blood for my sins. I believe that you rose again from the dead in three days and now I am receiving you as my personal savior, my lord, my only hope of salvation. I know that I am a sinner and deserve to go to hell, I know that I cannot save myself, Lord be merciful to me, a sinner and save me according to the promise of your word. I want Christ to come into my heart now to be my savior, lord and master. Amen. Congratulations if you accepted Jesus as your savior today. Now tell someone that you accepted Jesus into your heart and make it public. The bible says "If you are ashamed to confess me (Jesus) before man. I'll be ashamed to confess you before my father (God) in heaven. Read the word of God and you soon will find out just how much Jesus will begin to bless you each day. Amen.

Here are "8" steps to life's blessings, read and study them.

1. Belong to Gods family-JOHN 3:1-3
2. Keep his Commandments-TITUS 2:11-12
3. Humble yourself-JAMES 4:6
4. Give generously-2 CORINTHIANS 9:6-9
5. Love one another-JOHN 13:34-35
6. Strive for unity-PSALM 133
7. Forgive others-MARK 11:25-26
8. Give and it shall be given unto you, good measure, pressed down and shaken together-LUKE 6:38

God bless You and I will be praying for you as you grow in the love of Christ. Amen

SAUCERED AND BLOWED

Well folks it looks like were at the end of the book now, but your journey to recovery has just begun. Man doesn't it feel great to have some helpful information. Don't forget when you buy my book you will be spreading the gospel around the world. By the way "Saucered and Blowed was an old saying my grandpa would say to me when we were finished working for the day. It means we gotter done! Years ago people would pour their coffee onto a saucer and blow on it to cool it down. Anyway, folks it's been a pleasure to share some of my insight with you about anxiety/panic attacks, phobias and just plain ole fear. I just know that if you will apply what you have learned in this book, you will be able to get a grip on things a lot sooner than I did. I know that you will do it, I have faith in you. I will be praying that this information and hope will give you the strength to move on with your life and be extremely happy. God Bless and Thanks.